Health

Recipe	Page	Calories per serving	Fast	Sophisticated	Fat burner	For company	Inexpensive	Can make in advance	Easy	Rich in vitamins
Cardamom Chicken	6	168	●	●						
Chicken Breast with Pumpkin	6	166		●	●					
Tortilla Sandwich with Fish	8	333			●	●				
Herb Tomatoes with Pasta	10	346	●				●			
Flat Rice Noodles with Vegetables	10	401		●			●			
Penne with Asparagus and Arugula	11	340					●			●
Buckwheat Noodles with Salmon and Spinach	11	422		●						●
Chicken with Coconut Milk	12	471	●						●	
Duck Breast with Eggplant Rice	12	409					●		●	
Warm Turkey Salad with Nectarines	14	180							●	●
Warm Turkey Salad with Chinese Cabbage	14	170			●				●	
Thai Rice with Pineapple	18	323			●			●		
Citrus Curry with Blood Oranges	18	113						●		●
Filled Herb Crêpes	20	237		●				●		
Asparagus with Mozzarella	22	160	●							●
Saffron Vegetables	22	80							●	●
Asparagus Fondue and Tomato Salsa	24	214				●			●	
Asparagus with Tofu	24	165	●	●						
Stuffed Eggplant	26	144		●					●	
Potatoes with Herb Mousse	26	294					●		●	
Fennel with Baby Corn and Spinach	27	198					●			●
Fennel with Orange Juice	27	174							●	●
Red Cabbage with Chestnut Gnocchi	28	375		●				●		
Swiss Chard with Porcini Mushrooms	28	179	●						●	
Brussels Sprouts with Hazelnuts	30	146				●			●	
Salsify with Tofu	30	105				●			●	

R e c i p e

Guide

A wok is a good investment and as cooking techniques go, it's ideal for keeping your figure slim. Take advantage of ancient cooking wisdom for body shaping and fitness.

Wok Dishes are Automatically Low-Fat

Scientists consider Asian cuisine to be especially healthy and that is mainly due to the wok:
• Wok cooking requires very little oil, which is especially beneficial to your weight, physical fitness and arteries.
• Low-calorie vegetables prepared in the wok stay both crisp and delicious. The short cooking time due to high temperatures serves to preserve most of their healthy nutrients including vitamins, minerals, phytochemicals and fiber.

The Wok—a Favorite Tool of Healthy Cuisine

Wok dishes are guaranteed to make any dinner party into an event. You can also use it on a daily basis for your own meals. In addition to Asian specialties, try out some of the other fantastic international dishes in this book. You'll see how wonderful low-fat cooking can be when you take advantage of the variety of techniques discussed. Use these practical tricks and tips, from stir-frying and braising to red-braising and stewing, from blanching to steaming, all with a simple flick of the wrist.

Light Lunches

Tips for Buying a Wok

The wok used to be suspended directly in the fire. Today, different models are available.

- For gas stoves, you can buy the traditional rounded wok, which requires a ring base to keep it steady.
- Woks for electric stoves have a flat outer base and a rounded interior. They can also be used on gas stoves.
- Coated woks used for extra-low-fat cooking must be treated carefully. Overheating and scratching can damage the coating and ingesting the coating can be unhealthy. Once this happens, the oil no longer sticks well to the coated sides.
- Iron woks are the perfect universal pan for low-fat cuisine. They conduct heat almost instantly and are excellent for all low-fat cooking methods.
- Stainless steel or aluminum woks are good for steaming and as a spare or second wok.
- For low-fat steaming, you need a lid for your wok (usually made of aluminum).

Low-Fat Techniques

With the exception of deep-frying, all the cooking techniques using a wok are low-fat.

Starting Out Right

Always heat the wok first, then brush it with oil and bring both wok and oil back up to temperature.

Stir-frying

When you're tossing prepared ingredients in small amounts of oil that is very hot, a lot depends on your timing.

- So: Always have all the ingredients ready, including the stock or any other liquids, before you start cooking. Clean and chop your vegetables, meat, etc., ahead of time because you won't have time once the cooking begins. Cook the ingredients one at a time, quickly moving ingredients around with a wooden spatula or metal wok spatula and cook each ingredient in batches. Brown them briefly on the hot wok bottom and then push them up the sides (the higher up you go, the cooler the temperature) or let them drain on a rack (an internal rack if your wok has one or a standard kitchen rack) so you can cook them further later on.

Braising

Instead of oil, use a little stock or sauce and let the heat of the liquid cook your meats and vegetables. As with stir-frying, stir constantly with the spatula. If using stock, salt it at the very beginning.

Whereas stir-frying keeps everything crispy, braising makes everything slightly translucent and just a bit softer. In both cases, all the ingredients retain their color and flavor.

Stewing

You can also quickly brown the ingredients by stir-frying or braising and then cover and cook them over medium heat. When they are almost done, remove the lid, turn up the heat and reduce the sauce as much as you like.

Red-braising

After browning the meat, braise it in soy sauce. This gives it a darker color.

Blanching

Toss the vegetables into boiling, salted water. As soon as the water returns to a boil, pour out water and vegetables and rinse the vegetables under cold water, preferably in a colander. This will halt the cooking process.

Steaming

Steaming ingredients in a covered wok works like a charm.

- Dry-steaming above a boiling liquid is best done with a stainless steel insert. Asian bamboo baskets are also useful. Brush oil in the bottom of a basket, arrange the dry ingredients decoratively inside and you can then serve them in the same basket when done.
* For wet-steaming, the ingredients are marinated and then steamed in a steamer insert or a bowl placed on top of a stand.

Cardamom Chicken

● Sophisticated
● Fast

Serves 4

5 kohlrabi
(or 3 white turnips)
3 red bell peppers
4 onions
1 clove garlic
2 skinless chicken breast
fillets (about 10 oz)
³/4 cup stock
(basic recipe on page 17)
2 cloves
1 bay leaf
2 tsp flavored oil
(Szechuan peppercorn oil,
recipe on page 33)
¹/4 tsp ground cardamom
Salt and pepper

Prep time: 25 minutes

Per serving approx:
168 calories
22 g protein/3 g fat/
11 g carbohydrates

1 Clean and wash vegetables, peel if necessary. Cut kohlrabi into narrow strips about 2 inches long. Cut bell pepper into narrow strips and then cut in half horizontally. Peel onions and cut into thin rings. Peel garlic and grate finely. Cut meat into narrow strips.

2 Heat the wok. Over medium heat, bring to a boil 5 tbs stock, onions, cloves and bay leaf. Evaporate stock while stirring constantly.

3 Heat flavored oil in the wok once stock is gone. Toast garlic for 2 minutes. One at a time, add kohlrabi, bell peppers and chicken breast strips to the center of the wok and stir-fry. Add cardamom and fry all ingredients for 2 minutes. Add remaining stock, bring to a boil, cover and stew for 5 minutes, stirring occasionally. Season to taste with salt and pepper. Serve with bulgur wheat.

VARIATION

You can also prepare this dish with other vegetables that are in season. It tastes great with broccoli combined with salsify or asparagus.

> **TIP!**
> You can also prepare this dish with ¹/2 tsp curry powder instead of cardamom. Cardamom is one spice in curry powder, so if you like one you'll probably like the other.

Chicken Breast with Pumpkin

● Sophisticated
● Fat burner

Serves 4:

1 piece kabocha squash
(or pumpkin)
(about 1 pound)
2 apples (Fuji or red
delicious work well)
1 bunch cilantro or
Italian parsley
2 red onions
2 tsp flavored oil (chili oil,
recipe on page 33)
2 skinless chicken breast
fillets (about 10 oz)
Salt and pepper
³/4 cup stock
(basic recipe on page 17)
2 tbs light soy sauce

Prep time: 30 minutes

Per serving approx:
166 calories
19 g protein/3 g fat/
15 g carbohydrates

1 Wash squash, apples and cilantro and pat dry. Peel squash, remove seeds and cut into cubes of about 1 inch. Quarter the apples, remove cores and cut into wedges. Peel the onions, cut in half and then into narrow strips.

2 Heat the wok, then the oil. Sauté onions over medium heat until translucent. Season the chicken breasts with salt and pepper, add to the wok and sauté for 3 minutes until golden brown, then remove from wok.

3 Pour in the stock. Stir in squash and apples, bring to a boil and place chicken breasts on top. Cover and stew over low heat for 5–10 minutes, stirring occasionally.

4 Chop the cilantro finely and add to the wok. Season to taste with soy sauce, salt and pepper. Serve with rice or millet (page 17).

> **TIP!**
> Due to its small size, the aromatic kabocha squash is ideal for this recipe. New in recent years, the average kabocha is 2–3 pounds with a green skin and orange-red flesh. You can easily store it at home for two months.

Photo bottom: Cardamom
Chicken
Photo top: Chicken Breast
with Pumpkin

Flatbread Sandwich with Fish

● For company
● Fat burner

Serves 4:

For the tortillas:
4 oz whole grain flour
4 oz all-purpose flour
1 tsp salt
2/3 cup lukewarm water
Flour for the work surface

For the filling:
1 zucchini (about 8 oz)
1 bunch Italian parsley
1 large bunch arugula
8 leaves frisée or endive
1 1/2 oz alfalfa sprouts (optional)
4 cod fillets (about 4 oz each)
Salt and pepper
4 tsp peanut oil
1/2 cup sweet-and-sour sauce

Prep time: 1 1/4 hours
Standing time: 30 minutes

Per serving approx:
333 calories
25 g protein/10 g fat/
36 g carbohydrates

1 In a bowl, combine flour and salt. Make a well in the center, add 1/3 of the water and knead together with a little of the flour. Knead in remaining water about 1 tbs at a time until the all the flour is used and you have a workable dough.

2 Shape dough into a ball, place in a bowl, cover and let stand 30 minutes at room temperature.

3 In the meantime start the filling: Wash zucchini, parsley, arugula, frisée or endive and alfalfa sprouts (if any) and pat dry. Clean zucchini, grate finely, cover and set aside. Remove parsley and arugula leaves from stems.

4 Knead tortilla dough briefly and thoroughly, shape into a long cylinder and cut into 8 pieces. Shape each piece into a ball. On a floured work surface, roll out the dough into 8 thin tortillas (about 7 inches in diameter) and layer them on a floured dish towel, making sure they do not stick together.

5 Preheat oven to its lowest setting, about 150 degrees or "warm".

Heat the wok and fry tortillas one by one over medium heat 1 1/2 minutes on each side, moving them back and forth. Then wrap in a towel and place in the oven to keep warm.

6 Season fish fillets with salt and pepper, and dice. Reheat the wok, add the oil and heat. Sauté fish over medium heat in two batches for 4 minutes on each side until golden brown. Remove the fish when it is done, do not push it up the sides of the wok. Set aside and keep warm in the oven.

7 Cut each leaf of arugula and frisée or endive in half horizontally and then tear into bite-sized pieces. Lay out the tortillas on the work surface. Sprinkle grated zucchini over them, followed by the arugula. Top with fish sweet-and-sour sauce. Sprinkle with parsley and finish with the radicchio or endive.

8 Roll up tortillas, serve on dinner-sized plates and, if desired, garnish with alfalfa sprouts.

VARIATION

For the filling, you can also use chopped pork fillet. Brown pork for 3 minutes in 2 tsp garlic oil (recipe on page 33). In the wok, combine with 6 oz cooked bulgur wheat (half the recipe on page 17) and 2 tbs chopped parsley. Season with 2 tbs oyster sauce, salt and pepper. Roll up this mixture in tortillas along with 1 tbs chopped chives and 4 romaine leaves cut into strips.

Herb Tomatoes with Pasta

● Inexpensive
● Fast

Serves 4:

10 oz durum wheat pasta
Salt
4 oz frozen peas
2 pounds ripe, beefsteak tomatoes
1 chili pepper
2 tsp flavored oil (garlic oil, recipe on page 33)
1 bunch Italian parsley
2 sprigs mint
1 tsp honey
Pepper

Prep time: 30 minutes

Per serving approx:
346 calories
13 g protein/3 g fat/
67 g carbohydrates

1 Cook pasta according to directions on package in a large amount of salted water until al dente. Drain pasta and rinse with cold water. In ¹/₂ cup water, bring peas to a boil and drain remaining water.

2 Wash tomatoes, remove cores and cut into small cubes. Wash chili pepper.

3 Heat the wok, then the oil. Brown chili pepper over medium heat for ¹/₂ minute. Add diced tomatoes and stir-fry over high heat for 5 minutes.

4 Wash parsley and mint, shake dry and chop finely. Stir into tomatoes. Remove chili pepper with tongs or spoon. Stir in peas and pasta and season to taste with honey, salt and pepper.

Flat Rice Noodles with Vegetables

● Sophisticated
● For company

Serves 4:

8 oz flat rice noodles
Salt
6 oz green beans
1 red bell pepper
1 red onion
1 clove garlic
1 piece ginger (about 1 inch long)
4 tsp olive oil
10 oz broccoli florets
¹/₂ cup stock (recipe on page 17)
5 tbs dark soy sauce
2 tbs chopped cashews

Prep time: 25 minutes

Per serving approx: 401 cal.
15 g protein/8 g fat/68 g carb.

1 Cook noodles according to directions on package in salted water until al dente. Remove and rinse with cold water.

2 In the meantime, wash and clean vegetables. Chop beans and bell pepper. Peel onion, cut in half and then into narrow strips. Peel garlic and ginger and chop finely.

3 Heat the wok, then the oil. Stir-fry bell pepper over medium heat for 1 minute. A little at a time, add and beans and brown them. Add broccoli and onions and stir-fry until al dente.

4 Stir in garlic and ginger. Pour in stock and soy sauce and simmer 1 minute. Add noodles and cook until they are hot. Serve with cashews sprinkled over top.

Penne with Asparagus and Arugula

● For company
● Rich in vitamins

Serves 4:

10 oz penne	
Salt	
1 pound white asparagus	
2 tomatoes on the vine	
1 large bunch arugula	
1 clove garlic	
4 tsp olive oil	
Pepper	
Juice from 1/2 lemon	

Prep time: 25 minutes

Per serving approx:
340 calories
12 g protein/5 g fat/
62 g carbohydrates

1 Cook pasta according to directions on package in a large amount of salted water until al dente, then drain and rinse with cold water.

2 In the meantime, wash asparagus, peel and cut diagonally into thin slices. Wash tomatoes, remove cores and dice finely. Wash arugula, remove leaves from stems and chop into narrow strips. Peel garlic and mince.

3 Heat the wok, then the oil. Sauté asparagus over medium heat for 4 minutes, until al dente. Add the tomatoes and cook for 3 minutes. Stir in pasta and arugula, and season to taste with lemon or lime juice, salt and pepper.

Buckwheat Noodles with Salmon and Spinach

● Sophisticated
● Rich in vitamins

Serves 4:

10 oz buckwheat noodles	
Salt	
7–8 oz spinach	
2 scallions	
8–9 oz salmon fillet	
2 tsp peanut oil	
1/2 cup vegetable broth (basic recipe on page 17)	
2 tbs dark soy sauce	
Pepper	

Prep time: 25 minutes

Per serving approx: 422 cal.
22 g protein/13 g fat/
55 g carbohydrates

1 Cook noodles according to directions on package in a large amount of salted water until al dente, then drain and rinse.

2 In the meantime, wash spinach, pick out bad leaves, tear into small pieces and drain. Clean scallions, wash, cut 1/3 of the green part into fine rings and chop the rest. Cut salmon into 1 inch cubes.

3 Heat the wok, then the oil. Brown salmon over medium heat for 2 minutes. Stir in spinach and scallions (not the green part cut into rings). Season with soy sauce, toss, set aside and keep warm.

4 Bring stock to a boil in the wok. Stir noodles into stock and add to salmon. Season with salt and pepper and sprinkle with green onion rings.

Chicken with Coconut Milk

● Easy
● Fast

Serves 4:

10 oz orecchiette pasta
Salt
1 green chili pepper
1 leek (about 7 oz)
1 piece ginger
(about 1 inch long)
8 oz skinless chicken breast
Pepper
4 oz canned corn
1 bunch chives
4 tsp peanut or canola oil
1/2 cup stock
(basic recipe on page 17)
1/2 cup canned,
unsweetened coconut milk

Prep time: 30 minutes

Per serving approx:
471 calories
24 g protein/8 g fat/
75 g carbohydrates

1 Cook pasta according to directions on package in a large amount of salted water until al dente, then drain and rinse.

2 Wash chili pepper, clean, cut in half lengthwise, remove seeds and cut into fine strips. Clean leek, cut open lengthwise, wash and cut into strips. Peel ginger and chop finely. Cut chicken breasts into strips about 3/4 inch wide and season with salt and pepper. Drain corn. Wash chives, pat dry and chop.

3 Heat the wok, then the oil. Fry chicken breast strips over medium heat for 4 minutes until golden brown. Add leek to the center of the wok and cook for 2 minutes until translucent. Add chili pepper, ginger and corn and stir-fry for 2 minutes. Mix everything together.

4 Pour in stock and coconut milk, bring to a boil, cover and simmer for 3 minutes. Add pasta and heat. Season with salt and pepper and sprinkle with chopped chives.

VARIATION

For a special occasion, you can also add 6 oz unpeeled shrimp to this dish. De-vein shrimp along their back and stir-fry in the wok for 4 minutes before adding the chicken. Set aside and keep warm, then add the shrimp with the pasta.

Duck Breast with Eggplant Rice

● Easy
● For company

Serves 4:

2 eggplant
(about 1 1/4 pounds)
Salt
1 sprig mint
1 1/2 bunches chives
1 green chili pepper
1 small red onion or
2 shallots
10 oz skinless duck breast
4 tsp peanut or canola oil
1 1/4 pounds cooked rice
(recipe on page 17)
3 tbs balsamic vinegar
2 tbs dark soy sauce
Pepper
1 tbs honey

Prep time: 30 minutes

Per serving approx:
409 calories
19 g protein/19 g fat/
42 g carbohydrates

1 Wash eggplant, clean and cut into cubes of about 3/4 inches. Wash mint and chives and pat dry. Cut 5 mint leaves into strips and chop chives. Wash chili pepper, cut in half lengthwise, remove seeds and cut into strips about 1/4 inch wide. Peel onion or shallots and chop finely. Cut duck breast into narrow strips.

2 Heat the wok and then 2 tsp oil. Stir-fry eggplant over medium heat for 5 minutes. Add onion to the center of the wok and sauté until translucent. Stir in chili pepper, mint strips and rice, and heat. Season to taste with 2 tbs vinegar, soy sauce, salt and pepper. Remove and keep warm.

3 Reheat the wok and heat remaining oil. Stir-fry duck breast over medium heat for 3 minutes. Add honey and stir-fry for 1 minute. Pour in remaining vinegar.

4 Distribute duck breast over eggplant and rice mixture and serve sprinkled with chopped chives and remaining mint leaves. Goes very well with a warm baguette and tossed salad.

Photo bottom: Duck Breast with Eggplant Rice
Photo top: Chicken with Coconut Milk

Warm Turkey Salad with Nectarine

● Easy
● Rich in vitamins

Serves 4:

4 tsp peanut oil
Juice from 1/2 lemon
Salt and pepper
8 oz turkey cutlets
1 tbs finely chopped rosemary
2 oz radicchio
1/2 head Batavia or iceberg lettuce
4 nectarines

Prep time: 15 minutes

Per serving approx:
180 calories
17 g protein/6 g fat/
16 g carbohydrates

1 Combine 2 tsp oil with lemon juice, salt and pepper.

2 Cut turkey cutlets into strips about 1 inch wide and sprinkle with rosemary. Clean the lettuce, wash, pat dry and tear into bite-sized pieces. Wash nectarines, remove pits and cut into eighths.

3 Heat the wok, then the remaining oil. Stir-fry turkey strips over medium heat for 5 minutes until golden brown on all sides and drain on rack.

4 Stir-fry nectarine eighths in the wok for 2 minutes. Add turkey strips, cover and let stand briefly.

5 Toss salad with lemon dressing and transfer to plates. Distribute meat and nectarines over the top. Goes well with oven-warmed baguette, and baked or fried potatoes.

VARIATION

You can also make this dish with fresh figs, peaches or mango and, for a change, season the turkey breast with a Tandoori spice mixture. Adding 1–2 tbs sliced almonds will give it an extra, delicate aroma. First toast the almonds in the wok without oil and sprinkle them over the salad before serving.

Warm Turkey Salad with Chinese Cabbage

● Easy
● Fat burner

Serves 4:

1 small head Chinese cabbage (about 1 pound)
1/2 pineapple
1 small red onion
10 oz turkey cutlets
1 tsp Tandoori spice mixture (available at specialty markets)
Salt and pepper
1 bunch Italian parsley
4 oz sprouts (radish or alfalfa)
2 tsp honey
2 tbs rice wine vinegar
4 tsp flavored oil (Szechuan peppercorn oil, recipe on page 33)

Prep time: 30 minutes

Per serving approx:
170 calories
21 g protein/4 g fat/
13 g carbohydrates

1 Clean Chinese cabbage, cut into quarters, wash and cut into strips about 1 inch wide. Peel pineapple, remove core and dice. Peel onion, cut in half and then into narrow strips. Cut turkey cutlets into strips about 1/2 inch wide and season with Tandoori spices, salt and pepper. Wash parsley, pat dry and chop finely. Wash sprouts and drain.

2 Heat the wok and then caramelize the honey over medium heat until golden brown. Braise pineapple in honey for 2 minutes while stirring constantly, pour in vinegar and cook for 2 minutes. Remove from the wok and keep warm.

3 Heat 2 tsp oil in the wok. Sauté Chinese cabbage and onions until translucent. Briefly toss around in the wok with all but 1 tsp of the parsley and season with salt and pepper. Stir in pineapple, season to taste, set aside and keep warm.

4 Clean the wok, reheat and then heat remaining oil. Stir-fry turkey strips over medium heat for 4 minutes until golden brown.

5 Transfer Chinese cabbage to plates. Top with turkey strips, sprouts and remaining parsley.

Photo bottom: Warm Turkey Salad with Chinese Cabbage
Photo top: Warm Turkey Salad with Nectarines

Vegetarian Dishes

The beauty of your dishes depends on how you chop the ingredients.

Preparing Ingredients

You'll need a sharp knife or Asian cleaver to ensure that all the ingredients retain their shape. A sharp cut makes for crisp vegetables. Another important thing is to coordinate the sizes so that all the ingredients will finish cooking at the same time. This is the only way to prepare low-fat dishes in which everything remains crispy and juicy and they retain their vitamins and minerals.

How you chop the ingredients for cooking in the wok is up to you. Asian chefs have spent centuries trying different methods.

Chopping Techniques

Have fun experimenting with your knife or cleaver:
• Cut straight across for round slices or on an angle for ovals.
• For sticks, cut slices into pieces $1/2$ x $1/2$ x 2 inches; to julienne, cut into matchstick strips.
• For cubes, cut the strips straight across; for diamonds, cut strips on an angle.
• For an oblique cut, slice a carrot or cucumber diagonally, then roll it 180° and cut it diagonally on the same angle as before. Place your palm flat on the carrot and after each cut, roll it half way around. Then roll it back after the second cut.
• For textured edges, cut small lengthwise grooves in zucchini or carrots with a peeler or channel knife before slicing straight.

Ingredients can be chopped in a variety of ways to make for a decorative dish.

Basic Recipes for Wok Cooking

Cooked Rice

For 4 servings, rinse 10 oz rice under cold water until the water runs clear and soak in about 2 1/2 cups cold water for 15–30 minutes. In a pot, bring water and rice to a boil, stir, cover and cook over low heat.

Polished rice and the more nutritious parboiled rice cook in 20 minutes; fiber-rich whole-grain rice takes 20–45 minutes.

Wok Rice

You can also make rice in the wok. The water level should be 1 inch above the rice. Cover and cook, stirring occasionally.

Yellow Rice

For 4 servings, peel 1 onion, dice and cook in the wok in 1 tsp oil until translucent. Then cook 10 oz round-grain rice (Italian arborio) until translucent. Pour in 2 1/2 cup hot vegetable stock, bring to a boil and season with salt and 1/2 tsp turmeric. Cover and cook over low heat for 20 minutes, stirring occasionally.

Rice with Millet

For this Korean recipe, rinse 8 oz round-grain rice and 2 oz millet under warm water until the water runs clear (otherwise the millet might taste bitter). In the wok, combine rice and millet with 2 1/2 cups salted water and bring to a boil. Cover and cook over low heat for 20 minutes, stirring occasionally. Turn off heat and let steep for 15 minutes.

Bulgur

First heat the wok, then heat 4 tsp butter and stir in 1 tbs tomato paste. Add 10 oz bulgur and stir together. Pour in 3 cups water, season with salt and bring to a boil. Cook bulgur over medium heat while stirring for 10–15 minutes until all the liquid has evaporated.

Toasting Nuts

Heat the wok, then add the nuts and stir-fry for 5–10 minutes, depending on the amount, until golden brown. Be careful as nuts can go from brown to burnt very quickly. Remove and let cool.

Asian Chicken Stock

Using kitchen shears, cut about 2 1/2 pounds chicken legs and thighs into smaller pieces. Combine with 1 oz sliced ginger root, 1 peeled onion, 1/2 carrot, 6 (Szechuan) peppercorns and 2 quarts salted water. Cover and simmer over low heat for 1 hour. Pour stock through a strainer and use meat for Middle-Eastern Curried Rice with Vegetables (recipe on page 36).

Vegetable Stock

Peel 1 onion. Chop 4 oz leek, 4 oz celery and 8 oz carrot very finely. Coarsely chop 1 bunch parsley. Combine these ingredients with 1 bay leaf, 1 oz sliced ginger and black pepper. Add to a pot with 1 quart salted water and bring to a boil. Cover and simmer over low heat for 45 minutes, then strain. Divide into smaller portions and freeze.

These ingredients make a vegetable stock that can be used in many dishes.

Thai Rice with Pineapple

● Fat burner
● Inexpensive

In Thailand, this dish is called "galloping horses," because the Thai arrange the rice in a series waves over the pineapple slices, making it look like a row of jumps for horses. Try it out!

Serves 4:

2 scallions
1 carrot
1 red bell pepper
1 pineapple
1 oz cashews
2 tsp peanut oil
1 cup vegetable stock (basic recipe on page 17)
Salt and pepper
Pinch sugar
1 1/4 pounds cooked rice (recipe on page 17)
1 tbs freshly chopped mint

Prep time: 30 minutes

Per serving approx:
323 calories
6 g protein/7 g fat/
58 g carbohydrates

1 Clean and wash scallions. Cut white part in half and then into strips. Finely chop green part. Clean carrots, peel and cut into matchstick-sized strips. Cut bell pepper in half, clean, wash and cut into narrow strips. Peel pineapple, quarter lengthwise, remove core and cut into pieces about 3/4 inch thick.

2 Heat the wok, then toast cashews without oil over medium heat for 1 minute while stirring until golden brown. Remove from the wok and set aside.

3 Reheat the wok, then heat the oil. Sauté white part of scallions over medium heat for 1 minute until translucent. Add carrots and pepper strips to the center of the wok and stir-fry for 4 minutes until al dente. Pour in stock, bring to a boil and season with salt, pepper and sugar. Add the rice, making sure it is not in big clumps, stir and heat the entire dish. Stir in scallion greens.

4 Reassemble the pineapple onto plates, forming them in the shape of original, larger slices. Distribute rice over the top and garnish with mint and cashews.

Citrus Curry with Blood Oranges

● Inexpensive
● Rich in vitamins

Serves 4:

2 blood oranges
2 pink grapefruit
1 medium zucchini
2 green bell peppers
2 red onions
2 tsp flavored oil (garlic oil, recipe on page 33)
2 tbs curry powder
2 pinches Tandoori spice mixture (available at specialty markets)
1 1/4 cups vegetable stock (basic recipe on page 17)
Salt and pepper
1 tbs potato starch or
1 tsp carob flour

Prep time: 20 minutes

Per serving approx:
113 calories
3 g protein/3 g fat/
18 g carbohydrates

1 Peel oranges and grapefruit, also removing white membrane around covering flesh. Cut fruit lengthwise into wedges. Wash zucchini, clean, cut in half lengthwise and cut into slices about 1/4 inch thick. Cut bell peppers in half, clean, wash and cut diagonally into strips. Then cut the strips in half diagonally. Peel onions, cut in half and then into narrow strips.

2 First heat the wok, then the oil. Stir-fry onions over medium heat for 3 minutes until translucent. A little at a time, add bell peppers and zucchini slices to the center of the wok and stir. Dust with curry and Tandoori spices and sauté for 2 minutes, until al dente.

3 Pour in stock, bring to a boil and then season with salt and pepper. Stir potato starch into a little water and use to thicken the sauce (stir carob flour directly into sauce). Add fruit wedges just before removing from heat. Serve with rice and a tossed salad.

Photo bottom: Thai Rice with Pineapple
Photo top: Citrus Curry with Blood Oranges

Filled Herb Crêpes

● Inexpensive
● Sophisticated

Serves 4:

For the crêpes:
2 bunches Italian parsley
5 oz wheat flour
1/2 tsp baking powder
Salt
1 egg
$1/2$ cup low-fat milk
$1/4$ cup sparkling mineral water
4 tsp peanut oil
For the filling:
10 oz mushrooms
10 oz carrots
8 oz parsnip or celery
1 bunch scallions
1 tsp flavored oil (garlic oil, recipe on page 33)
$3/4$ cup vegetable stock (basic recipe on page 17)
Pinch cayenne pepper
Salt
2 tbs dark soy sauce

Prep time: 45 minutes
Refrigeration time:
20 minutes

Per serving approx:
237 calories
11 g protein/7 g fat/
33 g carbohydrates

1 Wash parsley, pat dry and chop finely.

2 Combine flour, baking powder and salt. Stir in egg, milk and mineral water with a wire whisk until you have a runny crêpe batter. If necessary, add more mineral water. Stir in parsley and refrigerate batter for 20 minutes.

3 Wash mushrooms, clean and cut into quarters. Clean carrots and parsnip, oblique cut (see page 16). Clean and wash scallions. Cut white part in half lengthwise and then into thin slices. Cut green part into pieces about $1/2$ inch long and set aside.

4 For the crêpes, pre-heat oven to 200°F or low setting. First heat the wok, then brush lightly with oil. With a ladle, pour one quarter of the crêpe batter into the wok. Cook crêpe on both sides until golden brown. Make all 4 crêpes, brushing the wok with oil before each one, and place in the oven to keep warm.

5 For the filling, reheat the wok, then the oil. Stir-fry scallion whites over medium heat for 3 minutes, until trans-lucent. If necessary, add a little vegetable stock. A little at a time, add carrots, mushrooms and parsnip to the center

of the wok and stir-fry for 2 minutes. Pour in vegetable stock and bring to a boil. Stir in scallion greens. Season to taste with cayenne pepper, salt and soy sauce.

6 Lay crêpes out flat on pre-warmed plates. Top each with filling and fold crêpe over the top. Goes with tossed salad dressed with lemon juice, salt and pepper.

VARIATION

For a special occasion, you can also serve this dish with an avocado lime sauce. Cut 1 avocado in half and remove the pit. Remove avocado from peel and chop. Using a hand blender or wooden spoon, purée with the juice of 1 lime and $1/4$ grated garlic clove. Season to taste with salt and pepper.

Green Asparagus with Mozzarella

● Fast
● Rich in vitamins

1¼ pounds asparagus
4 oz currants
¼ head frisée
1 bunch chives
1 small red onion or 2 shallots
1 plum tomato
8 oz Mozzarella
3 tsp olive oil

Prep time: 30 minutes

Per serving approx:
160 calories
14 g protein/9 g fat/
6 g carbohydrates

1 Wash asparagus, peel and cut diagonally into pieces about 1 inch long. Carefully wash currants, drain and remove berries from stems. Clean frisée, wash, pat dry, tear into small pieces and arrange on plates. Wash chives, pat dry and chop. Peel onion or shallots and mince. Finely chop tomato. Drain Mozzarella, cut into slices ¼ inch thick and distribute on dinner plates.

2 First heat the wok, then the oil. Stir-fry the asparagus over medium heat for 4 minutes. Add onions to the center of the wok and stir-fry 1 minute until translucent. Stir in tomatoes and season with salt and pepper. After 1 minute, stir in currants and cook everything for 1–2 minutes while stirring. Arrange on plates. Sprinkle with chives and serve with a baguette.

TIP!

If the currants are too sour, season dish to taste with honey. Because currants are extremely rich in fiber, they're ideal for healthy cuisine. For a change, you can also add 2–3 tsp hazelnut oil when you add the currants. Be careful of the fat content in Mozzarella. If you use the flavorful mozzarella di bufala, you'll need smaller portions.

Saffron Vegetables

● Easy
● Rich in vitamins

Serves 4:

1 small head cauliflower
2 carrots (about 6 oz)
1 zucchini (about 8 oz)
4 oz firm mushrooms
2 scallions
1 bunch Italian parsley
4 tsp flavored oil (chili oil, recipe on page 33)
5–7 saffron stems
1 sprig rosemary
Juice from 1 lemon
1 cup vegetable stock (basic recipe on page 17)
Salt and pepper

Prep time: 30 minutes

Per serving approx:
80 calories
4 g protein/4 g fat/
6 g carbohydrates

1 Clean cauliflower, wash and cut into small florets. Clean and peel carrots and clean zucchini. Cut both into sticks of about ½ x 1½ inches. Wash mushrooms, clean and cut in half. Clean and wash scallions. Cut green part into fine strips and set aside for garnish. Cut the rest into pieces about 1 inch long. Wash parsley, pat dry and chop finely.

2 First heat the wok, then the oil. Sauté white part of scallions until translucent. Add cauliflower and stir-fry for 3 minutes. A little at a time, add the other vegetables to the center of the wok and stir: Stir-fry carrots and saffron for 3 minutes until the carrots are al dente. Add zucchini and then mushrooms, rosemary and parsley. Add lemon juice and stock and bring to a boil. Simmer for 3 minutes. Season with salt and pepper and garnish with scallion greens. Serve with rice.

TIP!

Give this dish an Asian flavor by stirring in 1 tsp coriander seeds and 1 tbs grated ginger with the rosemary.

Photo bottom: Asparagus with Mozzarella
Photo top: Saffron Vegetables

Asparagus Fondue and Tomato Salsa

● Easy
● For company

Serves 4:

For the tomato salsa:
8 oz plum tomatoes
1 red onion
1/4 clove garlic
1 chili pepper
2 tbs honey
Juice from 1 lime
or 1/2 lemon
2 tbs vegetable stock
(basic recipe on page 17)
Salt and pepper
For the fondue:
4 pounds asparagus
2 large carrots
(about 12 oz)
12 oz small mushrooms
12 oz broccoli
1 quart vegetable stock
(basic recipe on page 17)
Salt and pepper
Chopsticks or wire ladle

Prep time: 30 minutes

Per serving approx:
214 calories
14 g protein/4 g fat/
30 g carbohydrates

1 Wash tomatoes, remove cores and quarter. Peel onion and garlic and mince. Wash chili pepper, halve lengthwise, clean and chop finely.

2 First heat the wok, then caramelize the honey until golden brown while stirring.

Braise onion, garlic, chili pepper and tomatoes in the honey for 1 minute. Pour in lime or lemon juice and stock. Season to taste with salt and pepper. Transfer to a bowl to cool.

3 Wash asparagus, peel the bottom 2 inches of the stalks and cut in half crosswise. Clean carrots, peel, cut into quarters lengthwise and cut in half crosswise. Wash and clean mushrooms. Wash broccoli, clean and cut into florets. Cut florets into sticks about 1/4 inch thick.

4 Heat the wok. Bring vegetable stock to a boil, season with salt and pepper and then simmer over low heat, preferably on an alcohol burner at the table. With chopsticks or wire ladles, hold vegetables in stock for 6–8 minutes until done. Serve with tomato salsa, pineapple ginger relish (recipe on page 33) and avocado lime sauce (recipe on page 20).

Asparagus with Tofu

● Sophisticated
● Fast

Serves 4:

2 pounds asparagus
10 oz baby corn
(fresh or from a jar)
2 red onions
1 bunch Italian parsley
6 oz tofu
4 tsp flavored oil
(Szechuan peppercorn oil,
recipe on page 33)
3/4 cup vegetable stock
(basic recipe on page 17)
1/4 cup dark soy sauce
Salt and pepper

Prep time: 30 minutes

Per serving approx:
165 calories
11 g protein/6 g fat/
16 g carbohydrates

1 Wash asparagus, peel and cut diagonally into pieces about 2 inches long. Halve the baby corn on an angle. Peel onions, halve and cut into narrow strips. Wash parsley, pat dry and chop finely. Cut tofu into small cubes.

2 First heat the wok, then the oil. Stir-fry onion strips over medium heat for 3 minutes until translucent. A little bit at a time, add asparagus and corn to the center of the wok and stir-fry until translucent. Pour in vegetable stock, bring to a boil, cover and stew for 6 minutes.

3 Stir in tofu, cover and bring to a boil again. Remove wok from heat. Season with soy sauce, salt and pepper. Stir in parsley. Serve with yellow rice or bulgur (recipes on page 17).

VARIATION

You can also use only half the asparagus and replace the other half with 8 oz snow peas or sugar-snap peas cut in half on an angle. You can then cook the peas with the corn. Or instead of asparagus, use cauliflower, broccoli or Romanesco cauliflower florets.

Photo bottom:
Asparagus with Tofu
Photo top: Asparagus
Fondue with Tomato Salsa

Stuffed Eggplant

- ● Sophisticated
- ● Easy

Serves 4:

1 eggplant
Salt
2 red onions
4 oz feta cheese (whole piece)
2 tsp oregano
Pepper
10 oz arugula
8 oz cherry tomatoes
2 tbs balsamic vinegar
2 tsp flavored oil (garlic oil, recipe on page 33)
6 tbs stock (basic recipe on page 17)

Prep time: 20 minutes

Per serving approx: 144 cal.
9 g protein/6 g fat/
13 g carbohydrates

1 Wash eggplant, clean, cut lengthwise into 8 thin slices and salt. Peel onions and dice. Cut feta into 8 slices.

Season with 1 tsp oregano and pepper. Pat eggplant dry, top with cheese and roll up. Wash arugula, clean and tear leaves from stalks. Wash tomatoes, cut in half and season with remaining oregano.

2 Brush eggplant rolls with 1 tsp flavored oil. Heat the wok and brush with 1 tsp oil. Brown eggplant for 3 minutes, adding 3 tbs stock. Remove from the wok and keep warm.

3 Heat remaining stock in wok. First add arugula, then tomatoes, and season with salt and pepper. Place eggplant rolls on serving plates and pour arugula mixture over top.

Potatoes with Herb Mousse

- ● Inexpensive
- ● Easy

Serves 4:

For the potatoes:
2 1/2 pounds small, firm potatoes (about 1 inch in diameter)
For the mousse:
1 bunch chives
1 bunch cilantro
1 bunch Italian parsley
10 oz low-fat yogurt
10 oz low-fat Quark (cheese)
Juice from 1 lemon
Salt and pepper

Prep time: 30 minutes

Per serving approx:
294 calories
19 g protein/1 g fat/
51 g carbohydrates

1 Wash potatoes, scrub well and cut larger potatoes in half lengthwise.

2 Pour enough water into the wok so that the steamer is directly above the water level. Bring water to a boil. Place potatoes in steamer, cover and cook over low heat for 25 minutes (if necessary, add more hot water). Peel potatoes with a towel by rubbing the skin off.

3 In the meantime, wash herbs, pat dry and chop finely. Purée with yogurt in a blender. Stir herb yogurt into quark using a wire whisk and season to taste with lemon juice, salt and pepper. Serve with potatoes. Goes with tossed salad and marinated herring.

Fennel with Baby Corn and Spinach

● Inexpensive
● Rich in vitamins

Serves 4:

1 pound fennel
6 oz baby corn
(fresh or from a jar)
6 oz carrots
4 oz spinach
10 oz cherry tomatoes
1 small red onion
2 cloves garlic
4 tsp flavored oil (chili oil, recipe on page 33)
Juice from 1 lime
Salt and pepper

Prep time: 30 minutes

Per serving approx: 198 cal.
7 g protein/5 g fat/
31 g carbohydrates

1 Wash and clean vegetables. Clean fennel, remove core and cut into narrow strips. Cut corn diagonally into 4 pieces. Peel carrots, cut them in half crosswise and then cut into thin sticks. Cut spinach leaves without stems into strips about 1 inch wide. Quarter tomatoes. Peel onion and cut into rings. Peel garlic and chop.

2 First heat the wok, then 3 tsp oil. Sauté onions over medium heat until translucent. A little at a time, add vegetables to the center of the wok: Stir-fry fennel and corn for 4 minutes and carrots for 1 minute. Toss tomatoes, garlic and spinach around in the wok. Season with lime juice, salt, pepper and remaining flavored oil. Goes well with rice.

Fennel with Orange Juice

● Rice in vitamins
● Easy

Serves 4:

1 pound fennel
8 oz cherry tomatoes
6 oz bean sprouts
12 oz arugula
4 peaches
2 tsp flavored oil (chili oil, recipe on page 33)
3/4 cup freshly squeezed orange juice
Salt and pepper
1 tbs honey
Dash of vinegar
Juice from 2 limes

Prep time: 30 minutes

Per serving approx:
174 calories
8 g protein/3 g fat/
28 g carbohydrates

1 Wash vegetables and fruit. Clean fennel, remove core and cut into narrow strips. Quarter tomatoes. Drain sprouts and arugula separately. Cut peaches in half, remove pits from and cut into wedges.

2 In the wok, bring the oil, orange juice and fennel to a boil. Reduce the liquid to half the amount. Stir in sprouts, season with salt and pepper, cover and bring to a boil.

3 Remove wok from heat. Season to taste with honey, vinegar, lime juice, salt and pepper. Stir in peaches and tomatoes. Distribute arugula and fennel on plates and spoon fennel mixture over top. Serve millet or yellow rice (recipe on page 17) as a side dish.

Red Cabbage with Chestnut Gnocchi

● Sophisticated
● Can make in advance

Serves 4:

For the gnocchi:
1 1/4 pounds Idaho potatoes
5 oz chestnuts
Salt
6 oz flour
1 pinch nutmeg
Pepper
4 tsp sunflower oil
For the red cabbage:
1 small red cabbage
(about 1 1/4 pounds)
1/2 mango without pit
2 onions
3/4 cup vegetable stock
(basic recipe on page 17)
2 tsp thyme leaves
Salt and pepper

Prep time: 1 hour

Per serving approx:
375 calories
10 g protein/5 g fat/
70 g carbohydrates

1 Wash potatoes, peel and cut into quarters. Using a small knife, score chestnut shells with a cross. In two different pots, cover potatoes and chestnuts with water, cover pots and cook over low heat for 20 minutes. In the case of the potatoes, salt the water.

2 Clean red cabbage, cut into eighths, wash, remove core and cut into narrow strips. Peel mango and cut into 1/2 inch cubes. Peel onion, cut in half and cut into narrow strips.

3 Pour water off potatoes and wait until they're cool enough to handle. Peel chestnuts. Purée both ingredients and add flour, nutmeg, salt and pepper. Shape mixture into 4 rolls about 1 inch thick and about 2 inches long and cut each piece into 6 smaller pieces. Press down on each piece with a fork.

4 Bring a large amount of salted water to a boil. Cook gnocchi until they rise to the top and then drain.

5 First heat the wok, then the oil. Sauté gnocchi over medium heat in batches, 2 minutes on each side. Set aside; keep warm.

6 Reheat the wok. Toss red cabbage and onions for 2 minutes. Pour in stock, stir in mango and simmer for 2 minutes. Season with thyme, salt and pepper. Serve with gnocchi.

Swiss Chard with Porcini Mushrooms

● Easy
● Fast

Serves 4:

Salt
4 oz glass noodles
1 tsp sesame oil
1 1/4 pounds Swiss chard
4 yellow onions
14 oz porcini mushrooms
2 tsp sunflower oil
Pepper
1/2 cup vegetable stock
(basic recipe on page 17)
1 tbs chopped cilantro
1/4 cup dark soy sauce

Prep time: 30 minutes

Per serving approx:
179 calories
10 g protein/4 g fat/
25 g carbohydrates

1 Bring a large amount of salted water to a boil and cook noodles for 5 minutes. Then pour into a colander, drain and mix with sesame oil.

2 Wash and clean Swiss chard. Cut stems only lengthwise into 1/4 inch strips and then cut the strips diagonally. Cut leaves lengthwise into eighths and then into narrow strips. Peel onions, cut in half and then into narrow strips. Wash mushrooms, clean and cut into eighths.

3 First heat the wok, then the oil. Sauté onions over medium heat for 2 minutes until translucent. Stir-fry mushrooms and chard stems for 3 minutes until the liquid has evaporated. Season with salt and pepper. Transfer vegetables to a bowl and keep warm.

4 In the wok, bring vegetable stock to a boil. Cook chard leaves for 2 minutes. Stir in warm vegetables and bring to a boil. Stir in noodles, cilantro or parsley, and soy sauce. Season to taste once again and serve hot. Serve with rice (recipe on page 17).

Photo bottom:
Red Cabbage with Chestnut Gnocchi
Photo top: **Swiss Chard with Porcini Mushrooms**

Brussels Sprouts with Hazelnuts

● Inexpensive
● Easy

Serves 4:

1¹/₄ pounds
Brussels sprouts
1 small chili pepper
4 red onions
8 oz sweet potatoes
1 tsp flavored oil (garlic oil, recipe on page 33)
1¹/₂ oz coarsely chopped hazelnuts
1¹/₄ cups vegetable stock (basic recipe on page 17)
Salt and pepper

Prep time: 30 minutes

Per serving approx:
146 calories
8 g protein/8 g fat/
10 g carbohydrates

1 Wash Brussels sprouts, clean outer leaves if needed and cut in half. Wash chili pepper, cut in half lengthwise, clean and cut into narrow strips. Peel onion and cut into eighths. Peel sweet potatoes and cut into cubes of about 1 inch.

2 First heat the wok and then brush with flavored oil. Stir-fry onions, chili pepper and hazelnuts over medium heat for 2 minutes until translucent. A little at a time, add Brussels sprouts and sweet potatoes to the center of the wok and stir for 1 minute.

3 Pour in vegetable stock and bring to a boil. Season to taste with salt and pepper. Cover and stew over low heat for 5 minutes, stirring occasionally. Serve with potatoes.

TIP!

This dish is pure health food. Brussels sprouts, chili peppers and sweet potatoes are all good for lowering cholesterol levels. The same applies to hazel-nuts if you eat them in small amounts, as in this recipe. When this combination of foods is prepared in a wok, you get a delicious meal that helps make you thin or stay that way!

Salsify with Tofu

● Inexpensive
● Easy

Serves 4:

¹/₂ pineapple (about 7 oz)
1 green bell pepper (about 7 oz)
7 oz tofu
1¹/₄ pounds salsify (or asparagus)
1 tsp flavored oil (Szechuan peppercorn oil, recipe on page 33)
1 tsp turmeric
³/₄ cup vegetable stock (basic recipe on page 17)
Juice from ¹/₂ lemon
1 tsp honey

Prep time: 20 minutes

Per serving approx:
105 calories
6 g protein/4 g fat/
9 g carbohydrates

1 Peel pineapple, cut into quarters and remove core. Cut quarters into ³/₄ inch cubes. Cut bell pepper in half, clean, wash and cut diagonally into strips about 1 inch long. Cut tofu into cubes of about ¹/₂ inch.

2 Wash salsify, scrub and peel carefully. Wash again thoroughly and cut diagonally into slices about ³/₄ inch thick.

3 Heat the wok, then brush on oil. Sauté salsify for 3 minutes until translucent. Add turmeric and then pour in vegetable stock. Bring to a boil and simmer for 3 minutes. Stir in bell pepper and pineapple and cook for another 3 minutes, stirring occasionally. Stir in tofu and lemon juice and season to taste with honey. Serve with bulgur, rice or potatoes.

VARIATION

Salsify can be difficult to find in many markets. Ask your natural foods store or produce clerk if they carry it. Most common time is summer and fall. If you cannot locate any, white or green asparagus will do wonderfully.

**Photo bottom:
Salsify with Tofu
Photo top: Red Cabbage
with Hazelnuts**

Spicing and flavoring are especially important in low-fat wok cooking. When you take away flavors that normally come from fat, you have to add them through spices or some other form.

Fresh and Spicy

• There are several types of chili pepper ranging from mild to very hot. The hottest part is the seeds. Adding a whole chili pepper to a dish and cooking it very briefly lends just a touch of heat.
• Ginger, peeled and chopped fresh, gives your dishes a zesty, hot flavor. Wrapped tightly in thick paper, fresh ginger keeps in the refrigerator for several weeks. Asian markets sell special ginger graters.
• Lemon grass releases its intense lemon flavor if you flatten its thick stem before chopping. You can also substitute lemon peel.
• Cilantro has a slight Asian flavor or if you prefer something slightly more mellow, you can substitute Italian parsley.
• Bean sprouts are often available fresh and can be kept in the refrigerator for 3–4 days in a permeable plastic bag. Canned bean sprouts will be crispier if you soak them in water in the refrigerator for 1 hour before cooking.

Fresh spices: Lemon grass, ginger, herbs and chili peppers.

Spicy Meat and Fish

Basic Oils

The high temperatures in a wok require heat-resistant oils, which is why refined canola oil is especially suited to this purpose.

Because canola oil has a neutral flavor, ingredients become nice and crispy but retain their original flavor.

Canola oil is good for both hearty and sweet dishes. It is also easy to flavor with spices using the recipes to the right. Because it contains 94% unsaturated fatty acids, canola oil is good for you from a nutritional and physiological standpoint. With its nutty flavor, cold-pressed canola oil is also ideal for cold dishes such as salads.

Basic Sauces

Soy, fish and oyster sauce are available just about everywhere. Here is a recipe for a more unusual sauce:

Pineapple Ginger Relish

This sauce goes well with vegetarian dishes and poultry. Finely dice 10 oz pineapple and 1 red onion. Finely grate about 1 inch of ginger. First heat the wok, then heat 1 tsp Szechuan peppercorn oil. Stir-fry pineapple, onion and ginger for 1 minute. Then add 2 tbs vegetable stock and 2 tbs rice wine vinegar. Season to taste with a pinch each of cinnamon, cayenne pepper and salt. Transfer relish to a bowl and let cool.

Homemade Flavored Oils

To make sure your flavored oils taste aromatic and fresh, prepare only small amounts and refrigerate.

Curry Oil

The day before preparing a dish, stir the amount of curry powder called for in the recipe into a little canola oil.

Garlic Oil

Peel 4 cloves garlic and slice. First heat the wok, then heat 1 tbs peanut or canola oil. Stir-fry garlic until golden brown, then let cool. Transfer to a screw-top jar and add 1/2 cup canola oil. Seal it tightly and it will keep for 3 weeks.

Chili Oil

First heat the wok, then stir-fry 3 tbs chopped, dried chili peppers in 1/2 cup peanut oil over low heat for 10 minutes. Marinate overnight in a screw-top jar, then strain and refrigerate. This oil will keep for 3 months.

Szechuan Peppercorn Oil

First heat the wok, then toast 2 tsp Szechuan peppercorns without oil over low heat for 1–2 minutes. Add 1/2 cup peanut or canola oil and cook for 5 minutes until the peppercorns are dark. Strain flavored oil and transfer to a screw-top jar. Use peppercorns for stews. Oil keeps for 2 months in the refrigerator.

A world of flavor: Oyster sauce (1), fish sauce (2), soy sauce (3), chili sauce (4), Szechuan peppercorn oil (5), curry oil (6), garlic oil (7), pineapple ginger relish (8)

Vietnamese Vegetables with Turkey

- Inexpensive
- Fat burner

Serves 4:

6 dried shiitake mushrooms
5 oz frozen peas
2 red onions
7 oz turkey cutlets
4 oz bamboo shoots
8 leaves of Chinese cabbage
1 red bell pepper
14 oz bean sprouts
4 tsp flavored oil (garlic oil, recipe on page 33)
Salt and pepper

Prep time: 35 minutes
Soaking time: 30 minutes

Per serving approx:
180 calories
22 g protein/5 g fat/
12 g carbohydrates

1 Cover mushrooms with warm water and soak for about 30 minutes. Remove stems and cut into quarters.

2 Thaw peas. Peel and halve onions. Cut onions, turkey and bamboo shoots into narrow strips.

3 Wash Chinese cabbage, pat dry and cut into strips the width of a finger and about 2 inches long. Cut bell pepper into quarters, clean, wash and cut into strips. Wash bean sprouts and drain.

4 First heat the wok, then 2 tsp flavored oil. Stir-fry turkey over medium heat for 5 minutes until golden brown and set aside.

5 Heat remaining flavored oil in the wok and stir-fry onions until translucent. Stir in bamboo shoots and stir-fry both ingredients for 7 minutes. Add Chinese cabbage to the center of the wok and braise all ingredients for 7 minutes. Season with salt and pepper.

6 A little at a time, add bell pepper strips, mushrooms, peas and bean sprouts to the center of the wok and stir-fry for 5 minutes until translucent. Stir in turkey. Serve immediately with fish sauce.

TIP!

For the sauce, dilute 3 tbs fish sauce concentrate with ³/₄ cup water and season with 2 tbs sugar and 1 tbs lemon juice.

Chicken Breast with Swiss Chard

- For company
- Fat burner

Serves 4:

8 oz skinless chicken breast fillet
10 oz Swiss chard
6 oz celery
2 shallots or
1 small red onion
1 clove garlic
2 blood oranges
2 tsp olive oil
1 tbs red wine vinegar
³/₄ cup chicken stock (basic recipe on page 17)
1 tbs dark soy sauce
Salt and pepper
1 oz chopped walnuts

Prep time: 30 minutes

Per serving approx:
220 calories
18 g protein/8 g fat/
17 g carbohydrates

1 Cut chicken breast fillet into strips. Wash and clean vegetables. Cut white part of chard diagonally into strips about ³/₄ inch long. Halve green part lengthwise and cut into strips. Slice celery. Peel and mince onions and garlic.

2 Peel oranges, including the white membrane that surrounds the flesh. Cut fruit into wedges.

3 First heat the wok, then the olive oil. Stir-fry chicken strips over medium heat for 4 minutes until light brown and drain on rack.

4 Sauté onions and garlic until translucent. Stir in chard and celery and sauté 4 minutes until translucent. Pour in vinegar, stock and soy sauce, cover and stew for 5 minutes, stirring occasionally.

5 Stir in oranges and chicken strips and season with salt and pepper. Let stand for 1 minute, then stir in walnuts and serve with rice.

Photo bottom: Vietnamese Vegetables with Turkey
Photo top: Chicken Breast with Swiss Chard

Middle-Eastern Curried Rice with Vegetables and Chicken

● Can make in advance
● For company

Serves 4:

For the stock:
2 chicken legs with thighs
1/2 onion
1/4 carrot
1/2 bunch parsley
Salt
2 black peppercorns
Pinch nutmeg
For the curried rice:
1 tsp flavored oil (curry oil, recipe on page 33)
2 oz orzo or crumbled spaghetti noodles
8 oz basmati rice
Salt
1/2 tsp curry powder
1/4 tsp cinnamon
For the vegetables:
8 oz frozen peas
10 oz potatoes
8 oz mushrooms
8 oz carrots
1 tsp flavored oil (chili oil, recipe on page 33)
2 tbs slivered almonds
Salt and pepper
For the finish:
1 tsp flavored oil (recipe on page 33)
3 oz raisins
Salt and pepper
1 tsp curry powder
Pinch cinnamon

Prep time: 50 minutes

Per serving approx:
500 calories
29 g protein/6 g fat/
82 g carbohydrates

1 Skin chicken legs and thighs and cut into smaller pieces. Peel onion and carrot. Place all these ingredients in 3 cups water with parsley, salt, pepper and nutmeg. Cover and simmer over low heat for 30–45 minutes. Pour stock through a strainer and take meat off bones. (Can be prepared in advance.)

2 First heat the wok, then 1 tsp curry oil. Sauté orzo (or spaghetti pieces) over medium heat for 5 minutes until brown, remove from heat.

3 In a pot, combine rice, pasta and 2 1/2 cups water. Season with salt, curry and cinnamon. Bring to a boil, cover and cook 25–40 minutes according to the directions on the rice package. (Can be prepared in advance.)

4 Thaw peas. Wash potatoes and scrub well. Wash mushrooms, clean and cut into sixths. Clean carrots, peel and cut into 1/4 inch slices.

5 First heat the wok, then 1 tsp chili oil. Toast almonds over medium heat until golden brown, then remove. Brown mushrooms in the wok until liquid has evaporated. Season with salt and pepper, remove from the wok and keep warm. (Can be prepared in advance.)

6 In the meantime, peel potatoes and cut into cubes of about 1/2 inch. Heat the wok, then 1 tsp flavored oil. Stir-fry potatoes for 3 minutes. Make a hole in the middle of the potatoes and gradually pour in 1/2 cup of the stock. Stir in carrots and peas, braise for 5 minutes, then season with salt and pepper. The carrots should be al dente. Remove from the wok and keep warm.

7 Reheat the wok and heat 1 tsp flavored oil. Stir-fry raisins for 1 minute. Add 1/4 cup chicken stock and chicken meat. Season with salt, pepper, curry and cinnamon. Stir in curried rice. Stir in vegetables, mushrooms and as much of remaining stock as desired. Sprinkle with almonds and serve with hot flat bread.

Lamb Fillet with Oyster Mushrooms

● Easy
● For company

Serves 4:

1 pound snow peas
1 pound oyster mushrooms
2 red onions
1 stalk lemon grass
4 tsp flavored oil (garlic oil, recipe on page 33)
1¹/₂ oz buckwheat (or millet)
4 tbs stock (your choice; basic recipes on page 17)
Salt and pepper
8 lamb fillets
4 tbs dark soy sauce

Prep time: 30 minutes

Per serving approx:
360 calories
48 g protein/10 g fat/
18 g carbohydrates

1 Clean and wash snow peas. Wash mushrooms and remove thick stems. Peel onions, cut in half and then into narrow strips. Pound lemon grass with knife handle to flatten it. Then slice thinly.

2 First heat the wok, then 2 tsp flavored oil. Stir-fry onions and buckwheat over medium heat for 3 minutes until translucent. Add mushrooms and stir-fry for 3 minutes. Stir in snow peas and stir-fry

everything together for 2 minutes. If necessary, pour in a little stock. Season to taste with salt and pepper. Remove from the wok and keep warm.

3 Reheat the wok and heat remaining oil. Fry lamb fillets and lemon grass over medium heat for 4 minutes. Pour in soy sauce and bring to a boil. Remove wok from heat, cover and let fillets stand for 4 minutes.

4 Add vegetables, stir and serve with potatoes or baguette.

> **TIP!**
>
> Mushrooms add flavor to low-fat cuisine. Cultivated mushrooms such as oyster mushrooms, shiitake, white mushrooms and porcini are less likely to contain harmful substances than wild mushrooms.

Pork Fillet with Oyster Sauce

● Easy
● Sophisticated

Serves 4:

1¹/₂ green bell peppers
7 oz small mushrooms
4 red onions
1 bunch scallions
10 oz pork fillet
4 tsp flavored oil (garlic oil, recipe on page 33)
Salt and pepper
1¹/₄ cups oyster sauce

Prep time: 30 minutes

Per serving approx:
202 calories
22 g protein/6 g fat/
18 g carbohydrates

1 Cut bell pepper in half, clean, wash and cut diagonally into strips about 1 inch long. Wash mushrooms, clean and cut into quarters. Peel red onions, cut in half and then into strips. Clean and wash scallions. Cut white parts in half lengthwise and cut into smaller pieces. Cut green parts into pieces about 1 inch long. Thinly slice pork fillet.

2 First heat the wok, then 2 tsp flavored oil. Stir-fry bell peppers, onions and white parts of scallions over

medium heat for 3 minutes. Add mushrooms to the center of the wok and cook everything for another 2 minutes while stirring. Season with salt and pepper. Transfer vegetables to a bowl and keep warm.

3 Heat the wok and then remaining flavored oil. Brown meat for 4 minutes while stirring. Pour in oyster sauce. Stir in scallion greens and vegetables and bring to a boil. Serve with rice.

> **TIP!**
>
> Red onions are excellent for wok preparations. They have a mild flavor and tender consistency, meaning that they don't taste too strong and they cook quickly. The same can be said of scallions, a favorite in Asian cuisine. Both the green and white parts should be used in most cases.

**Photo bottom: Lamb Fillet with Oyster Mushrooms
Photo top: Pork Fillet with Oyster Sauce**

Sliced Lamb with Bell Peppers

● Easy
● Sophisticated

Serves 4:

1 pound lamb loin
5 oz celery
1 red bell pepper
1 yellow bell pepper
1 small red onion
2 tsp sunflower oil
1 tbs curry powder
1 tsp freshly grated ginger
Salt and pepper
Pinch cayenne pepper
2/3 cup vegetable stock
(basic recipe on page 17)
4 sprigs mint

Prep time: 30 minutes

Per serving approx:
185 calories
27 g protein/7 g fat/
4 g carbohydrates

1 Trim fat from lamb loin, slice thinly and refrigerate.

2 Wash celery, clean and slice thinly. Cut bell peppers in half, clean, wash and cut diagonally into strips about 3/4 inch long. Peel onion, cut in half and then into narrow strips.

3 First heat the wok, then 1 tsp oil. Sauté lamb slices over medium heat until pink. Transfer to a plate, cover and keep warm.

4 Reheat the wok and then remaining oil. A little at a time, add celery and bell peppers to the center of the wok and sauté over medium heat for 3 minutes until translucent. Season with curry, ginger, salt, pepper and cayenne pepper. Pour in stock, bring to a boil, cover and simmer over low heat for 8 minutes, stirring occasionally.

5 Wash mint, pat dry and chop finely. Stir mint and lamb fillet into vegetables and heat for 3 minutes. Serve with rice.

VARIATION

Give this dish a tasty accent by replacing the curry powder with 1/4 tsp ground cardamom, 2 tsp turmeric and 1 tsp freshly grated ginger.

Beef Fillet with Cauliflower

● Easy
● Sophisticated

Serves 4:

1 pound beef fillet
3 tbs Tandoori spice mixture (available at specialty markets)
1 small head cauliflower
2 tomatoes on the vine
1 zucchini (about 6 oz)
1 small red onion
2 scallions
4 tsp sunflower oil
1/3 cup stock
(basic recipes on page 17)
1/2 cup unsweetened coconut milk (canned)
Salt and pepper

Prep time: 30 minutes

Per serving approx:
194 calories
24 g protein/8 g fat/
5 g carbohydrates

1 Cut fillet into cubes of about 1/2 x 1 inch and season with Tandoori spices. Clean vegetables and wash. Divide cauliflower into small florets and cut stems into small slices. Remove cores from tomatoes and dice finely. Cut zucchini into narrow sticks about 1 inch long. Peel red onion, cut in half and then into narrow strips. Clean and wash scallions. Cut white parts in half lengthwise and then into pieces about 1 inch long. Cut green parts into pieces about 1 inch long.

2 First heat the wok, then 2 tsp oil. Stir-fry meat over medium heat for 2 minutes and transfer to a plate.

3 Reheat the wok and then remaining oil. Sauté red onion until translucent. Add cauliflower and stir-fry for 3 minutes. Pour in stock and coconut milk and bring to a boil. Simmer for 5 minutes. Season with salt and pepper. A little at a time, stir in white part of scallions, zucchini and tomatoes and simmer for 3 minutes.

4 Stir diced fillet into vegetables, heat briefly, season to taste and serve on plates with scallion greens and rice.

Photo bottom: Beef Fillet with Cauliflower
Photo top: Sliced Lamb with Bell Peppers

Spinach Rice with Meatballs

● Inexpensive
● Easy

Serves 4:

2 red onions
1 pound spinach
3 tomatoes
6 oz lean ground beef
2 tsp chopped parsley
Salt and pepper
1 tsp tomato catsup
2 tsp olive oil
1/2 cup stock
(basic recipes on page 17)
1 1/4 pounds cooked rice
(basic recipe on page 17)
1 tsp Hungarian paprika

Prep time: 40 minutes

Per serving approx:
266 calories
17 g protein/24 g fat/
40 g carbohydrates

1 Peel onions, cut in half and mince. Sort spinach, wash, drain and cut into strips about 1/2 inch wide. Wash tomatoes, remove cores and dice finely.

2 Combine ground beef with parsley, salt, pepper and catsup. Shape into long rolls and then cut into small pieces, then shape into cherry-sized balls.

3 First heat the wok, then 1 tsp oil. Brown meatballs over medium heat for 4 minutes while stirring. Remove meatballs from the wok and keep warm.

4 Reheat the wok. Heat remaining oil and stir-fry onions until translucent. Stir in spinach in small batches. Stir in meatballs and diced tomatoes. Separate rice grains and add along with stock. Bring to a boil and season to taste with salt, pepper and paprika. Cover and let stand 1 minute. Serve with yogurt (stirred until smooth and seasoned with salt and dill) and warm flat bread.

Duck Strips with Baby Corn

● Easy
● For company

Serves 4:

For the marinade:
1 small chili pepper
2 tsp rosemary
1 tbs honey
2 tbs dark soy sauce
Juice from 1 lime
Salt
For the dish itself:
10 oz skinned duck breast
8 oz cherry tomatoes
7 oz snow peas
6 oz baby corn
(fresh or from a jar)
1 red onion
4 tsp olive oil
1/3 cup stock
(basic recipes on page 17)
1/3 cup dark soy sauce
Pinch Szechuan pepper
Salt and pepper

Prep time: 40 minutes

Per serving approx:
433 calories
31 g protein/20 g fat/
63 g carbohydrates

1 Wash chili pepper, cut in half lengthwise, clean and chop very finely. Chop rosemary finely. Combine both with honey, soy sauce and lime juice. Cut duck breast into strips. Combine with marinade and cover.

2 Clean and wash vegetables. Core tomatoes and cut into sixths. Cut snow peas in half diagonally. Cut baby corn lengthwise into thirds. Peel onion, cut in half and then into strips.

3 First heat the wok, then the oil. Brown duck strips for 4 minutes while stirring, remove and keep warm. Sauté onions in the wok until translucent. A little at a time, add vegetables to the center of the wok. Brown corn briefly. Stir-fry snow peas until al dente. Stir in tomatoes. Then stir-fry everything for 4 minutes.

4 Stir in stock and soy sauce, bring to a boil, cover and stew for 5 minutes. Season to taste with Szechuan pepper, salt and black pepper. Stir in duck strips. Serve with rice or pasta and tossed salad.

VARIATION

Instead of duck breast, use 14 oz lean beef or pork. Turkey fillet is also ideal, or de-boned dark meat chicken.

Photo bottom: Spinach Rice with Meatballs Photo top: Duck Strips with Baby Corn

Shrimp with Spinach

● Easy
● Fast

Serves 4:

1 pound spinach
1 zucchini (about 6 oz)
1 scallion
8 oz strawberries
14 oz raw, peeled shrimp
3 tsp olive oil
1 tsp sesame oil
Salt and pepper
2 tbs rice wine vinegar

Prep time: 30 minutes

Per serving approx:
183 calories
24 g protein/6 g fat/
24 g carbohydrates

1 Sort spinach, wash, remove thick stems and drain. Wash zucchini, clean and cut into thin sticks about 1½ inches long. Clean scallion, wash and chop. Set aside a little of the green part. Wash strawberries, remove stems, clean and cut into quarters. Wash shrimp and pat dry.

2 First heat the wok, then the olive oil. Stir-fry shrimp over medium heat for 3 minutes and drain on the rack. Stir-fry scallions and zucchini strips for 1 minute until translucent. Add spinach and sesame oil and season with salt and pepper. Mix together, sprinkle with vinegar and toss. Distribute on plates and sprinkle with strawberries, shrimp and remaining scallion. Serve with yellow rice (recipe on page 17) and warm flat bread.

TIP!

For this recipe be sure to use raw shrimp. The cooked shrimp that are commonly available become leathery in the wok.

Mussels with Bay Leaves

● Fat burner
● Sophisticated

Serves 4:

6 pounds mussels
6 oz carrots
6 oz celery
6 oz red onions
1 bunch scallions
1 tsp flavored oil (garlic oil, recipe on page 33)
2 cups vegetable stock (basic recipe on page 17)
4 bay leaves
Salt and pepper

Prep time: 45 minutes

Per serving approx:
122 calories
12 g protein/4 g fat/
9 g carbohydrates

1 Wash and scrub mussels. Press the open mussel shells together and hold for a few seconds. If they pop back open, discard (they're spoiled).

2 Wash and clean vegetables. Peel carrots. Coarsely chop carrots and celery. Peel onions. Clean and wash scallions. Chop both types of onion coarsely.

3 First heat the wok, then the flavored oil. Stir-fry red onions over medium heat until translucent. Add scallions, carrots and celery to the center of the wok and stir-fry for 4 minutes until translucent. Add bay leaves. Pour in stock, bring to a boil and season with salt and pepper.

4 Stir in mussels, cover, bring to a boil and then simmer for 12 minutes, stirring occasionally. Discard any mussels that did not open while cooking (they're spoiled). Serve mussels with vegetables in shallow bowls. Goes with yellow rice (recipe on page 17).

Photo bottom:
Shrimp with Spinach
Photo top: Mussels
with Bay Leaves

Steamed Trout with Green Sauce

● Easy
● Fat burner

Serves 4:

For the trout:
2/3 cup vegetable stock (basic recipe on page 17)
4 trout fillets
Salt and pepper
2 red onions
1 tsp peanut or canola oil
For the sauce:
1 bunch Italian parsley
1 bunch chives
1 bunch cilantro
1 1/4 cups buttermilk
Juice from 1/2 lemon
Salt and pepper

Prep time: 20 minutes

Per serving approx:
225 calories
38 g protein/6 g fat/
3 g carbohydrates

1 In the wok, bring stock to a boil. Sprinkle trout fillets with salt and pepper. Peel onions and cut into thin rings. Top trout fillets with onion rings.

2 Brush steamer with oil and fill with trout fillets. Place steamer in the wok directly above the stock. Cover and steam trout fillets for 8–10 minutes.

3 In the meantime, make the sauce: Wash parsley, chives and cilantro, pat dry and chop finely. Purée with buttermilk in a blender. Season to taste with lemon juice, salt and pepper.

4 Distribute trout fillets on plates and surround with sauce. Goes with boiled potatoes or rice and a tossed salad.

TIPS!

If you want the sauce to be a little thicker, purée 1 medium cooked potato in the blender together with the herbs.

After steaming, freeze remaining stock for a fish soup.

Steamed Fish Fillets over Bean Sprouts

● Fat burner
● Sophisticated

Serves 4:

14 oz Swiss chard
7 oz bean sprouts
1 bunch scallions
Salt and pepper
2/3 cup vegetable stock (basic recipe on page 17)
1 tsp peanut or canola oil
4 whitefish fillets (cod, each fillet about 5 oz)

Prep time: 30 minutes

Per serving approx:
163 calories
31 g protein/3 g fat/
5 g carbohydrates

1 Clean and wash chard. Cut white part diagonally into strips about 1 inch long. Cut leaves in half lengthwise and then into narrow strips. Wash bean sprouts and drain. Clean and wash scallions. Cut white parts into fine rings. Cut green parts in half lengthwise. Season with salt and pepper.

2 In the wok, bring vegetable stock to a boil. Blanch scallion greens for about 1 minute, remove and pat dry with a paper towel. Remove wok from heat.

3 Form bean sprouts into equal-sized piles and tie up with onion greens. Brush bottom of steamer with oil. Place sprout bundles in steamer and fish on top.

4 In the wok, heat chard and white part of scallions in the stock. Place steamer over the stock, cover and steam fish for 10 minutes. Remove steamer and season chard to taste with salt and pepper.

5 Transfer chard and liquid to plates. Distribute bean sprout bundles on plates with fish on top. Goes with potatoes, sweet potatoes or rice and pineapple ginger relish (recipe on page 33).

Photo bottom:
Steamed Fish Fillets over Bean Sprouts
Photo top: Steamed
Trout with Green Sauce

Sole with Broccoli and Glass Noodles

● Easy
● For company

Serves 4:

3 sprigs cilantro
1 piece ginger
(about 1/2 inch)
Juice from 1 lime
1 tsp grated lime
or lemon peel
Salt and pepper
8 sole fillets
(about 2 oz each)
7 oz glass noodles
1 tsp sesame oil
2 scallions
3 tsp olive oil
1 pound broccoli florets
2/3 cup vegetable stock
(recipe on page 17)
5 tbs soy sauce

Prep time: 35 minutes
Marinating time: 1 hour

Per serving approx:
340 calories
28 g protein/6 g fat/
43 g carbohydrates

1 Wash cilantro, pat dry and chop finely. Peel ginger and grate. Combine herbs and ginger with lime juice, grated peel, salt and pepper. Cut sole fillets crosswise into strips about 1 inch wide and marinate in this mixture for 1 hour.

2 After 45 minutes, preheat oven to its lowest setting. Bring a large amount of salted water to a boil and cook glass noodles for 5 minutes. Drain and mix with sesame oil.

3 Clean and wash scallions. Cut white part into 1/2 inch pieces. Chop green part finely and set aside.

4 First heat the wok, then 2 tsp olive oil. Stir-fry fish over medium heat for 4 minutes until golden brown and transfer to oven to keep warm.

5 In the wok, heat remaining olive oil. Stir-fry broccoli over medium heat for 3 minutes until translucent. Add white part of onions to the center of the wok and stir-fry with broccoli for 2 minutes. Pour in stock and bring to a boil. Season with soy sauce, salt and pepper. Stir in noodles. Arrange with sole strips and onion greens.

Fillet of Sole with Chinese Cabbage

● Fat burner
● Sophisticated

Serves 4:

1 pound Chinese cabbage
1 red onion
2 cloves garlic
9 oz potatoes
1 piece ginger
(about 1/2 inch)
1 bunch basil
1 chili pepper
8 sole fillets
(about 2 oz each)
4 tsp olive oil
Salt and pepper
2 tbs flour
4 tbs dark soy sauce
1 pinch nutmeg
1 tbs chopped chives

Prep time: 30 minutes

Per serving approx:
190 calories
21 g protein/5 g fat/
15 g carbohydrates

1 Clean Chinese cabbage, wash and cut diagonally into strips. Peel onion, cut in half and then into narrow strips. Peel garlic and mince. Wash potatoes, peel and dice. Peel ginger and grate. Wash basil, pat dry and chop finely. Wash chili pepper, cut in half lengthwise, clean and chop finely. Cut each fish fillet into 3 pieces.

2 First heat the wok, then 2 tsp oil. Stir-fry potatoes until golden brown, transfer to a plate and keep warm.

3 Sprinkle fish with salt and pepper, dredge in flour and shake off excess. Reheat the wok and then 1 tsp oil. Sauté fish for 3 minutes, stirring gently, then set aside and keep warm.

4 Reheat the wok and then remaining oil. Stir-fry Chinese cabbage. Add onions to the center of the wok and stir-fry everything for 2 minutes. Stir garlic, chili pepper, ginger and basil into Chinese cabbage. Season to taste with soy sauce, nutmeg, salt and pepper. Distribute on plates. Cover with fish and potatoes. Serve with chives sprinkled on top.

**Photo bottom: Sole with Broccoli and Glass Noodles
Photo top: Fillet of Sole with Chinese Cabbage**

The Wok's Sweet Secrets

By the time dessert comes around, you're probably asking yourself "Can I afford to eat a little more?" You can if you stick to low-fat treats.

The Low-Fat Formula

According to dieticians, 25–30% of our daily allowance of calories should be calories from fat. But the diet books which subscribe to this theory are full of recipes which require too much time and energy. It's easier to start with your daily fat allowance and break this down to what you consume per meal:
• When a vegetable dish with a higher fat content is served with rice, it becomes a low-fat main dish.
• A salad with cold-pressed oil is good for you. If you eat fruit for dessert regularly, you'll keep the meal within your fat allowance.

Calculate in Grams, not Percentages

To stay slim, you need to maintain a daily fat intake of 55–75 grams. Consuming a total of 40–50 grams will allow you to lose weight.

• Half the fat you consume is "hidden" in many foods; the other half therefore, is contained in spreads and the fat used for cooking.
• To make sure this "hidden" fat doesn't exceed 27–37 grams, buy only low-fat products.
• To get a rough idea of "visible" fats, think in tsp (1 tsp=5 grams):
1 tsp for breakfast
2–3 tsp for lunch
2–3 tsp for dinner

Tip:
As they do in Italy, serve bread with your meals. It's low in fat and fills you up.

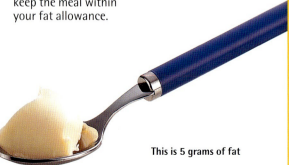

This is 5 grams of fat

Low-Fat Weekend

How about a three-day menu of low-fat food from the wok? Try out the suggestions below just for fun, including the Asian breakfast.

This delicious chicken soup fits almost every occasion:

Asian Chicken Soup

To serve 4, place 4 oz bean sprouts in a colander and pour boiling water over the top. In the hot wok, heat 1 tsp chili oil (recipe on page 33) and 2 cups chicken stock (include cooked, diced chicken if desired). In this liquid, heat 10 oz cooked rice. Transfer the sprouts to bowls and pour soup over the top. Sprinkle with 1 tbs chopped chives and garnish with thin lemon slices.

Tip:

Consume lots of vitamins and fiber in the form of fresh fruit, lettuce and bread. If you exceed your fat allowance for one day, try to make it up within the week, otherwise you'll quickly lose track.

Three-Day Menu

Day 1
Morning
• Orange halves
• Asian chicken soup (recipe on left) with a rye roll

Lunch
• Potatoes with herb mousse (p. 26) and tossed salad
• Seasonal Fresh Fruit

Evening
• Fennel with orange juice (page 27)
• Lamb fillet with oyster mushrooms (page 38) and salad
• Potato noodles with plums (page 56)

Snacks:
• Fruit from the wok is delicious and easy to prepare: To serve 4, heat the wok and caramelize 2 tbs honey. Add and stir-fry wedges from 1 apple, 1 peach and 2 kiwi for 30 seconds. Serve with a little yogurt. Other delicious combinations are: Slices from 1 banana or orange, 4 oz strawberries and wedges from 2 pears or finally 4 oz plums, wedges from 2 nectarines, and 6 oz pineapple or 4 oz strawberries.

Day 2
Morning
• Banana pancakes (page 58) with maple syrup and fruit salad

Lunch
• Tossed salad
• Duck breast with eggplant rice (page 12)
• Seasonal fresh fruit

Evening
• Asparagus fondue and tomato salsa (page 24)
• Cherry ragout with scrambled pancakes (page 60)

Snacks:
• Rye crostini with eggplant purée: Score 2 eggplant (about 1 pound) with a knife, steam in the wok for 20 minutes, purée and season with 1 tbs vinegar, 1 tsp soy sauce, 2 tsp garlic oil, salt, pepper and 1 shallot.

Day 3
Morning
• Milk rice with mangoes (page 59)

Lunch
• Tossed salad
• Flat rice noodles with vegetables (page 10)
• Seasonal fresh fruit

Evening
• Vegetables with green sauce (page 46)
• Fillet of sole with Chinese cabbage (page 48)
• Polenta sticks with raspberry purée (page 52)

Snacks:
• Warm poppy seed turnovers (page 52) with fruit salad

Beverage Tip:
Green tea is a fat burner. Drinking 4 cups a day helps keep off unwanted pounds. Drinking 1 1/2 to 2 quarts of water a day is also a great way to stay fit and healthy.

Your weekend promises a lot of variety!

Warm Poppy Seed Turnovers with Mango Sauce

- ● Easy
- ● Fat burner

Serves 4:

For the filling:
3/4 oz poppy seeds
1/2 cup low-fat milk
1 tbs honey
3 apricots
For the dough:
1 tsp sunflower oil
1 1/2 tsp dry yeast
1/2 tsp baking powder
Pinch salt
4 oz wheat flour
2 tbs honey
1/4 cup lukewarm water
3 tsp butter
Baking parchment paper
For the mango sauce:
1 mango
2 tbs honey
Juice from 1 lime

Prep time: 30 minutes
Rising time: 30 minutes

Per serving approx:
263 calories
6 g protein/6 g fat/
46 g carbohydrates

1 In a pot, bring milk and poppy seeds to a boil. Stir in honey, cover and simmer for 10 minutes. Remove from heat and let stand for 20 minutes. Wash apricots, remove pits and dice finely.

2 Line steamer with baking parchment, pierce several times and brush with oil. For the dough, mix yeast, baking powder, salt, flour, honey, water and butter with a hand mixer. Divide dough into 12 balls.

3 Stir apricots into poppy seed mixture. Make an indentation in each of the dough balls, insert a little of the poppy seed filling and close the balls over it.

4 Place turnovers in the steamer, spacing them out sufficiently, cover and let rise in a warm location for 30 minutes.

5 Pour enough water into the wok so that the steamer is directly above the water level and bring water to a boil. Place turnovers above the water, cover and steam for 15 minutes.

6 Peel mango and remove pit. Purée along with honey, lime juice and 3 tbs water. Serve poppy seed turnovers with mango sauce.

Polenta Sticks with Raspberry Purée

- ● Can make in advance
- ● Rich in vitamins

Serves 4:

For the polenta sticks:
2 cups low-fat milk
3 oz honey
6 oz coarse polenta
Pinch Bourbon vanilla
3/4 oz flour
2 tbs sunflower oil
For the raspberry purée:
10 oz raspberries
1 1/2 oz honey
Juice from 1 lime

Prep time: 30 minutes

Per serving approx:
353 calories
8 g protein/7 g fat/
63 g carbohydrates

1 In the wok, bring milk and honey to a boil while stirring with a wire whisk. Gradually add polenta and vanilla while stirring constantly and simmer over low heat for 2 minutes while continuing to stir.

2 Line a wide, flat pan or tray with plastic wrap. Spread out polenta in a layer about 1/2 inch thick, smooth the surface and let cool. Clean the wok.

3 In the meantime, purée raspberries with honey, lime juice and 6 tbs water. Put through a strainer to remove the seeds.

4 Cut polenta into finger-sized sticks of about 1/2 x 1/2 x 2 inches and dredge in flour. Shake off excess flour.

5 Preheat oven to its lowest setting. First heat the wok, then the oil. Fry sticks in 3 batches over medium heat for 2–3 minutes until golden brown and transfer to the oven to keep warm. Serve with purée.

TIP!

You can prepare the polenta the day before and fry prior to serving. Instead of raspberry purée, serve raspberry sauce: Purée 1 avocado, 8 oz raspberries, the juice of 2 limes, 2 oz honey and 1/2 cup water.

Photo bottom:
Polenta Sticks with
Raspberry Purée
Photo top: Warm Poppy
Seed Turnovers with
Mango Sauce

Pineapple Compote with Buckwheat

● Inexpensive
● Easy

Serves 4:

For the buckwheat:
4 oz buckwheat groats (grains)
2/3 cup low-fat milk
Salt
Pinch cinnamon
Pinch cardamom
1 tsp grated orange peel
For the pineapple compote:
1/2 pineapple
4 oz acacia honey
Pinch Bourbon vanilla
6 tbs passionfruit juice
6 tbs freshly squeezed orange juice
Juice from 1/2 lemon
1 tsp grated lemon peel
2 tsp potato flour or carob flour

Prep time: 20 minutes

Per serving approx:
250 calories
4 g protein/1 g fat/
5 g carbohydrates

1 First heat the wok, then toast buckwheat groats without fat for 4 minutes while stirring constantly until they begin to give off an aroma.

2 In a pot, bring milk to a boil with salt, cinnamon, cardamom and orange peel. Stir in buckwheat, cover and simmer over low heat for 20 minutes.

3 Peel pineapple, quarter, remove core and cut into cubes about 1/2 inch thick.

4 Clean the wok, reheat and heat the honey. Caramelize until golden brown while stirring constantly. Add vanilla and pineapple cubes and fry for 3 minutes while stirring constantly. Pour in all of the juice, stir in lemon peel, bring to a boil and simmer for 3 minutes.

5 Stir potato flour into water and stir into stewed pineapple to thicken. Distribute buckwheat on plates and serve with stewed pineapple.

TIP!

You can also make pineapple compote with kaffir lime leaves, available from Asian markets. You'll find carob flour in health food stores: This type of flour doesn't need to be stirred into water beforehand.

Pineapple Skewers with Cinnamon Quark

● Inexpensive
● Easy

Serves 4:

For the pineapple skewers:
1/2 pineapple
2 tsp peanut oil
16 wooden skewers
For the cinnamon quark:
1 pound sweetened quark (0.2% fat)
6 tbs honey
Juice from 1 lime
1/2 tsp cinnamon

Prep time: 30 minutes

Per serving approx:
198 calories
17 g protein/2 g fat/
28 g carbohydrates

1 Peel pineapple half, cut in half lengthwise and remove core. Halve both pieces again lengthwise and then cut crosswise into 8 equal-sized pieces. Stick 2 pineapple pieces on each wooden skewer.

2 Stir together quark, honey, lime juice and cinnamon until smooth.

3 First heat the wok, then brush with oil for each batch of skewers. Add 8 skewers at a time with the points downward and fry for 2 minutes on each side until golden brown. Transfer pineapple skewers to plates and serve with cinnamon quark.

VARIATION

You can also alternate mango and pineapple pieces on the skewers. Instead of the quark, stir together 8 oz cottage cheese and 1 pound low-fat yogurt until smooth and season to taste with spices.

TIP!

You can prepare the cinnamon quark ahead of time. You can also combine it with pineapple compote (recipe on this page) or cherry ragout (page 60), which can also be prepared in advance.

Photo bottom:
Pineapple Skewers with Cinnamon Quark
Photo top: Pineapple Compote with Buckwheat

Potato Noodles with Plums

● Inexpensive
● Easy

Serves 4:

For the plums:
18 oz plums
1 tbs rosemary
4 oz honey
1/3 cup currant juice
For the potato noodles:
10 oz Idaho potatoes
Salt
1 egg
2 tbs whole-grain flour
2 tbs semolina
Flour for the work surface
2 tsp butter

Prep time: 45 minutes

Per serving approx:
246 calories
4 g protein/3 g fat/
48 g carbohydrates

1 Wash plums, drain, remove stems, cut in half and remove pits. Wash rosemary, pat dry and chop.

2 First heat the wok, then caramelize the honey while stirring constantly until golden brown. The honey will start to give off an aroma and thicken slightly but should remain liquid.

3 Stir in plums and rosemary and braise while stirring. Pour in juice and bring to a boil. Cover and simmer over low heat for 8 minutes, stirring occasionally. Transfer to a bowl.

4 In the meantime, wash potatoes for the potato noodles, peel and quarter. Barely cover potatoes in the wok with salted water, bring to a boil, cover and cook over low heat for 20 minutes. Pour off water and wait until they're cool enough to handle.

5 Put potatoes through a ricer and let cool slightly in a bowl. Then knead thoroughly together with egg, whole-grain flour and semolina to form a soft potato dough and season to taste with salt.

6 On a floured work surface, shape dough into a roll about 1/2 inch in diameter and cut into pieces about 2 inches long.

7 In a pot, bring a large amount of salted water to a boil. Flour your hands and roll pieces of dough between them to make the dough pointed at the ends.

8 Carefully place potato noodles in gently simmering salted water and let cook for 5 minutes until they rise to the top. Remove with a slotted spoon and rinse under cold water.

9 Clean the wok and heat. Heat butter and fry potato noodles in two batches until golden brown, stirring carefully.

10 Arrange potato noodles and warm plums on plates and serve.

TIP!

Instead of plums, you can serve the potato noodles with cherry ragout (page 60). They also make an excellent side dish for hearty meat and poultry dishes. In this case, season the dough to taste with 1 pinch nutmeg. Instead of 10 oz potatoes, use 14 oz and add 2 tbs flour.

Melons with Glass Noodles

- Inexpensive
- Rich in vitamins

Serves 4:

1–2 Charentais
(or Honeydew) melons
(about 1 pound)
1 piece ginger
(about 1 inch)
1 oz honey
3 oz glass noodles
Pinch Bourbon vanilla
Juice from 2 limes
8 mint leaves

Prep time: 20 minutes

Per serving approx:
108 calories
3 g protein/1 g fat/
23 g carbohydrates

1 Cut melons in half, remove seeds, peel, cut into 1/2 inch cubes and place in the freezer.

2 In the meantime, peel and grate ginger. Heat 11/2 cups water in the wok. Bring to a boil with ginger and 2 tbs honey. Add noodles, cover and simmer over low heat for 3 minutes. Remove from heat. Stir in ginger. Let noodles absorb liquid, transfer to a shallow bowl so they won't stick together and refrigerate.

3 In a blender, purée melon with remaining honey and lime juice and transfer to shallow bowls.

4 Carefully separate noodles and place in the center on top of melon purée. Wash mint leaves, pat dry with a paper towel and garnish noodles with mint leaves.

Banana Pancakes

- Inexpensive
- Easy

Serves 4:

Pinch salt
Pinch cinnamon
5 oz flour
1 cup unsweetened
coconut milk (canned)
2 tbs honey
2 bananas
2 eggs
4 tsp peanut or canola oil
Juice from 1/2 lemon

Prep time: 40 minutes
Standing time: 1/2–1 hour

Per serving approx:
248 calories
8 g protein/6 g fat/
40 g carbohydrates

1 Using a hand blender, mix salt, cinnamon, flour, coconut milk and honey to form a

pancake batter and let stand 1/2–1 hour.

2 Peel bananas. Chop 1 banana finely and mix into batter along with eggs. (If the batter becomes too thick, stir in a little carbonated water). Slice second banana and stir into batter.

3 Preheat oven to its lowest setting. First heat the wok, then brush with oil. One at a time, using 1 ladleful of batter for each, fry 4 pancakes over medium heat until golden brown on both sides and transfer to the oven to keep warm. Brush the wok with oil before each pancake. Sprinkle pancakes with lemon juice and serve.

Milk Rice with Mangoes

● Easy
● Fat burner

Serves 4:

4 oz round–grain rice
2 ripe mangoes
1 1/4 cups unsweetened
coconut milk (canned)
3 tbs honey
1/2 tsp salt

Prep time: 30 minutes

Per serving approx:
190 calories
2 g protein/1 g fat/
43 g carbohydrates

1 Preheat oven to its lowest setting. In the wok, bring rice and 1 cup water to a boil. Cover and simmer over low heat for 20 minutes, stirring occasionally. Remove from heat, cover and place in the oven for 20 minutes until all the liquid has been absorbed.

2 Cut mangoes in half and remove pits. Score fruit to the skin with a knife in a grid pattern. Press in on peel side with your thumbs to pop the flesh side out.

3 In a pot, combine coconut milk, honey and salt. Bring to a boil while stirring and combine with rice. Serve on plates with mangoes. Serve warm or cold.

Coconut Soup

● For company
● Rich in vitamins

Serves 4:

3 oz glass noodles
2 tbs grated coconut
1 pomegranate
2 oranges
1 cup unsweetened
coconut milk (canned)
1 1/4 cups low-fat milk
1 pinch cardamom
5 saffron stems
2 tbs honey
2 tsp potato flour

Prep time: 35 minutes

Per serving approx:
197 calories
6 g protein/3 g fat/
36 g carbohydrates

1 Pour boiling water over noodles and let soak for 30 minutes.

2 Heat the wok and toast coconut until golden brown.

3 Cut pomegranate in half and remove seeds. Wash oranges under warm water, dry and grate off 1 tsp peel. Peel oranges, including white membrane covering flesh. Cut fruit into wedges, saving any juice that escapes.

4 Reheat the wok. Bring to a boil coconut milk, milk, cardamom, saffron, orange peel, orange juice and honey. Cover and simmer over low heat for 8 minutes. Stir potato flour into a little water and use to thicken the soup slightly.

5 Drain noodles, chop and stir into soup. Serve with oranges and pomegranate seeds.

Cherry Ragout with Scrambled Pancakes

● Inexpensive
● Easy

Serves 4:

For the pancakes:
3 oz whole wheat flour
3 oz all-purpose flour
Salt
1 cup low-fat milk
Grated peel from 1/4 lemon
2 eggs
4 mint leaves
4 tsp carbonated mineral water
5 tsp peanut or canola oil
For the cherry ragout:
1 1/4 pounds black cherries
1 cup cherry juice
Pinch Bourbon vanilla
2 tbs honey
2 small sticks cinnamon
2 tsp potato flour

Prep time: 45 minutes
Standing time: 1/2–1 hour

Per serving approx:
396 calories
10 g protein/15 g fat/
54 g carbohydrates

1 Combine flour, salt, milk and lemon peel and let this batter stand for 1/2–1 hour.

2 In the meantime, wash cherries for the cherry ragout, cut in half and remove pits.

3 In a pot, heat juice and season with vanilla and honey. Add cinnamon sticks and cherries, bring to a boil and simmer over low heat for 3 minutes. Stir potato flour into a little water and use to thicken stewed fruit slightly. Remove cinnamon sticks. Let cherries cool in a bowl.

4 Separate eggs. Stir 2 egg yolks into batter. Beat 1 egg white until stiff. Wash mint, pat dry and chop into strips. Beat batter with carbonated water. Fold in 1 tsp oil, mint and beaten egg whites.

5 Preheat oven to its lowest setting. First heat the wok, then the remaining oil. One at a time, fry 4 pancakes on both sides over medium heat. After turning, tear apart with two forks, fry until golden brown and transfer to the oven to keep warm. Serve with cherry ragout.

"French Toast" with Oranges

● Inexpensive
● Easy

Serves 4:

4 slices whole wheat bread
4 oz low-fat milk
1 egg
Salt
4 tbs honey
4 oranges
Pepper
1 tbs mint leaves
2 tbs breadcrumbs
2 tbs grated coconut
2 tsp sunflower oil

Prep time: 20 minutes

Per serving approx:
240 calories
6 g protein/7 g fat/
37 g carbohydrates

1 Cut bread slices diagonally to make 4 triangles of each. Arrange on a platter.

2 Whisk together milk, egg, salt and 2 tbs honey. Pour this mixture over bread slices and let them absorb it.

3 Peel oranges including white membrane covering flesh. Slice, being careful to save the juice. Place orange slices on a plate.

4 First heat the wok, then caramelize remaining honey over medium heat while stirring constantly. Brown orange slices on both sides and add orange juice. Season with pepper and cook for 2 minutes while stirring.

5 Wash mint leaves, pat dry and chop into strips. Remove orange slices from the wok and transfer to plates. Stir mint leaves into juice, reduce while stirring and pour into a bowl.

6 Combine bread crumbs and grated coconut. Take bread triangles from egg milk mixture and dredge in crumbs.

7 Clean the wok, reheat and brush with oil. In two batches, fry bread slices on both sides until golden brown. Serve with oranges and reduced juice.

Photo bottom: "French Toast" with Oranges
Photo top: Cherry Ragout with Scrambled Pancakes

Credits

Published originally under the title Wok Low Fat © 2001 Gräfe und Unzer Verlag GmbH, Munich. English translation for the U.S. market © 2002, Silverback Books, Inc.

Editors: Jonathan Silverman and Stefanie Poziombka
Translator: Christie Tam
Reader: Maryna Zimdars
Layout, typography and cover design: Heinz Kraxenberger
Typesetting and production: Patty Holden and Verlagssatz Lingner
Cover photo: Michael Brauner, Stockfood Eising
Photos: Odette Teubner

Printed in Hong Kong

ISBN 1-930603-17-7

Elisabeth Döpp
Döpp has long been a reader for large publishing companies and has been a cookbook author and health trainer in nutrition, with an emphasis on vegetarian and high nutrition cuisine, since 1985.

Christian Willrich
Willrich comes from Alsace and has been a chef in gourmet restaurants since 1980. His fine natural cuisine has met with great success for over 20 years.

Jörn Rebbe
Rebbe was trained as a chef in a Japanese hotel. He is now a chef specializing in Japanese and Chinese cuisine.

Odette Teubner
Teubner grew up among cameras, flood lights and experimental kitchens. She received her education from her father, the internationally known food photographer Christian Teubner.

ABBREVIATIONS	
oz =	ounce
tsp =	teaspoon
tbs =	tablespoon